THE AMAZING

DIRT

BOOK

written by
PAULETTE BOURGEOIS
with Valerie Wyatt

illustrated by
CRAIG TERLSON

ADDISON-WESLEY PUBLISHING COMPANY, INC.

Reading, Massachusetts   Menlo Park, California   New York

Don Mills, Ontario   Wokingham, England   Amsterdam   Bonn

Sydney   Singapore   Tokyo   Madrid   San Juan

Acknowledgements

The real dirt on dirt is that it would have been impossible without the help of the ever-patient staff at the Ontario Science Centre, Royal Ontario Museum and the North York Library System. All of my questions from "how many dust mites live in a double bed?" to "how does a city under a city get buried?" were answered in detail in record time. The Ontario Ministry of the Environment, Parks Canada and Brampton Brick provided valuable information about soil, sand and brick-making. I am grateful to Dr. Martin Morrice for reading the manuscript and making many valuable comments. I am especially grateful to Valerie Wyatt who plodded through the mud with me and shaped this book.

"The Dirt Under Your Bed," page 14, adapted from *The Secret House*, copyright © 1986 by David Bodanis, by permission of Simon and Schuster, Inc.

Originally published in Canada by Kids Can Press, Ltd., Toronto, Ontario.

ISBN 0-201-55096-2

Edited by Valerie Wyatt
Interior design by Nancy Ruth Jackson
Front cover illustration by Fred Hirsch/Carol Bancroft & Friends
Back cover illustration by Craig Terlson
Set by Alphabets

ABCDEFGHIJ-AL-943210
First printing, July 1990

CONTENTS

Dirt is everywhere. It's in the air, under your bed, covering the earth's crust and between your toes. You probably spend a lot of time trying to get rid of the dirt in your life. Still, dirt is important. It's even good for you. Read on for a few dirty surprises.

The dirt on dirt

Everything you want to know, need to know, and never thought of asking. Turn to page 38.

Dirt on the move

Hold on tight! The oceans are getting bigger. Africa is going one way. America is going the other. The Himalayas are getting taller. And it's all happening right under your toes. Turn to page 52.

You and dirt

Those greeby things are sleeping in my bed? You're kidding, right? Turn to page 14.

Buried!

Pssssst. Some people think they know where to find buried treasure. Just watch out for the booby traps. They're killers.
Turn to page 29.

Dirt homes

Does living in dirt sound disgusting? Not to an earthworm or a mole. Turn to page 56.

Bake a mud cake. Make a step in time. Stun your friends and family with amazing tunnel trivia and great archaeological wonders of the world. Grow a hideaway and build an adobe fort. MORE, MORE, MORE in *The Amazing Dirt Book.*

MORE MORE MORE!

CHAPTER 1

You And DIRT

So you just had a shower and you think you're pretty clean, right? Wrong! The second you step out of the shower, you start getting dirty again. Here's where the dirt hides — and how your body tries to fight it off.

Your scalp makes an oil that lubricates your skin and hair. Dirt clings to the oil.

Dirt tries to sneak into your ears, but they have a natural dirt protector. Ear wax traps the dirt before it reaches your delicate inner ear.

Grime tries to blow into your eyes, but your body fights back. First your eyelashes flap up and down to repel the dirt. If that fails, you turn on your windshield wipers — you blink.

Take a deep breath of dirty air and your nose goes to work. It's lined with tiny hairs that filter out dirt so it doesn't get into your lungs.

Sweat gets trapped in your belly-button and lint from your clothes sticks to it. The result: belly-button fluff.

Your nails are real dirt-grabbers. If you scratch an open cut, you could put germy dirt from your nails into the cut. If you put a dirty finger-nail into your mouth, you might be giving dirt, germs and even tiny parasites a ride into your body. The only solution? Scrub those nails.

Dirt sticks to wet spots. When your feet sweat, the dirt grabs on. Now why do you suppose dirt gathers between your toes?

Warning

Don't read this chapter if you have a weak stomach. There is so much gunk under your nails and between your toes that you may spend the rest of the day in the tub. There are so many greeby things lurking in dust that you may go crazy cleaning. And if you think water cleans dirt, you'd better read on. Dirt is tough stuff.

TAKE A BATH

People living in Crete 4000 years ago were as clean as we are today — they had flush toilets, hot and cold running water and baths. Around 600 BC the Phoenicians were scrubbing up with soap made from wood ash and goat fat. And for years, the Romans invited the whole town to communal baths. But then things got dirty.

By 500 AD most of the baths and pipes in the Roman Empire were smashed by invading barbarians. It was the end of cleanliness for another thousand years. People had a bath when they were baptized (and even then they wore their clothes because of religious prudery) and perhaps never again.

Everybody stunk! But the rich people doused themselves

in sickening sweet perfumes to cover the stench. The doctors of the time had a superstition: Washing would make people sick. They were wrong: Dirt makes a nice home to bacteria so disease was everywhere.

It wasn't until 1830, when a deadly disease called cholera killed millions in Europe, that people started cleaning up their act. Not only did people start washing . . . but they stopped emptying their chamber-pots out the windows and onto the heads of passers-by. There were toilets and sinks everywhere. Everyone realized that clean people not only smell better, they stay healthier.

Mud-baths

Have you ever thought of getting dirty to stay clean? It sounds backwards, but rhinos, pigs and elephants all do it. The mud gets rid of ticks and fleas and helps the animals stay cool. When the layer of mud dries hard, it helps protect the animals from the hot sun.

It's not only the animals who wallow in the mud. Amazingly, a lot of people will spend a fortune and travel around the world to sit in mud-baths. Every year 600 000 tourists flock to the Dead Sea to coat themselves in stinky, coal-black mud. The mud bakes in the hot sun and gets hard. Underneath, the body warms up, and aches and pains melt away. Dead Sea mud is supposed to be a cure-all for acne, psoriasis and even wrinkles. What's in the magic mud? A mix of minerals including feldspar, quartz, calcite, magnesium, and sodium, bromide and chlorine salts.

GETTING THE DIRT OUT

You can scrub as long as you like with plain water, but never get yourself clean. Here's why: Water is only good for getting things wet and washing things away. Each drop of water has a weak electrical charge that makes it attractive to other water molecules. Water molecules cling together and act as if they're covered in a thin layer of Saran Wrap. This is called surface tension, and it makes it impossible for water to get in and around tiny bits of dirt. To get rid of the dirt, we use soap with water. Soap breaks up the surface tension of water. The soap makes the dirt slippery so it loosens its grip on your skin and gets washed away in the water.

The first soap

Long ago the Phoenicians discovered that boiling goat fat, water and ash until the liquids evaporated made a hard, waxy soap. Soap-making around the world followed the same recipe until a lucky accident during the American Civil War. Procter and Gamble had been making a nice-smelling, pure white soap. It was called White Soap and it wasn't anything special — until a worker forgot to turn off his machines during his lunch break. When he came back from lunch, the soap was all whipped up, and the extra air in the mixture made the soap float. Buyers went crazy; they loved the Ivory soap because it didn't get lost in the tub.

Soap is wonderful stuff, but it has its drawbacks. It leaves a scum, for one thing. During the First World War, the Germans couldn't get fat into the country to make soap. They needed something to wash with, so they invented detergent, a "soapless soap" made from chemicals. To everyone's surprise, detergent was better than soap. There was no scum and it cleaned greasy dirt on hair and clothes.

All the dirt that's fit to print

Some people get so fed up reading newspapers and ending up with grimy, black hands that they wear gloves when they read. There is one advantage to having ink come off the page readily — it makes recycling newspapers easier.

Put your dirty clothes into a washing machine full of water and detergent and what happens? The soapy water whooshes in and out of each clothing fibre. The detergent molecules surround each piece of dirt and tug it away. The dirt-surrounded-by-soap floats into the wash water. The dirt can't cling to other fibres because it is too slippery to stick.

Tough dirt

When you try to clean a protein stain made by spilled blood, eggs or meat, you need extra cleaning power. Protein dirt is hard to get at. It's made of long, tangled chains. You need special enzyme detergents to cut through the chains to loosen them. Enzymes "eat" the dirt much as enzymes in your stomach "eat" your food.

Nit picking

Some people think only dirty people get head lice. Wrong. Lice don't know dirty from clean, poor from rich, old from young. Lice like heads. They wait around on combs, pillows, hats and head-rests on trains, planes and buses for a head. Any head. If you get head lice, don't worry. There are special shampoos that kill the lice and their nits — the eggs — in just one wash.

HEADS UP, TAILS DOWN!
HOW DO DETERGENT MOLECULES WORK?

Each detergent molecule has two ends. One end loves water and the other end hates water but loves grease, dirt and oil. When detergent is put into water, the water-loving ends stick into the water and the water-hating ends stick out of the water.

This breaks up the invisible skin on the water. The water can't stick together so it's free to move in and out of the tiny dirty holes in the fabric. While some of the detergent molecules hold the fort and prevent the water molecules from ganging up together, the rest of the detergent molecules grab bits of dirt and pull them off the fabric and into the water. Nasty business going on in your washing machine!

Detergent molecules are fast workers. As soon as they hit water, they start to arrange themselves with their water-loving ends down and their water-hating ends up! You can see how quickly detergent molecules do this in this experiment.

  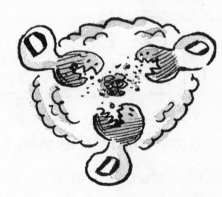

You'll need:
*two different colours of food
      colouring*
a cereal-sized bowl of milk
a large spoonful of detergent

1. Pour a few drops of each colour of food colouring into the milk. Don't stir.

2. Gradually pour some detergent along the side of the bowl and watch the colours explode.

DIRT UNDER YOUR BED

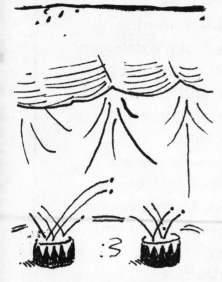

Some little kids are terrified of what's hiding under their bed. They imagine ghouls and trolls, witches and dragons. A hug and a night-light usually make the monsters disappear. Good thing they don't know about all the really disgusting stuff under their beds. No matter where you live, you'll find volcanic ash, garden soil, sea salt, car exhaust, flakes of skin, bits of tire meltings, cat flea eggs, bits of fibre and grit from bricks and stone — even African sand. There are 300 000 things floating in every cubic foot of air, over your bed, under your bed and around your bed.

How does African sand get in your bedroom? Desert sand comes in different sizes. A grain can be as large as 1 mm ($1/_{25}$ of an inch), or as small as 0.0001 mm ($1/_{2500}$ of an inch). Light breezes roll the middle-sized grains of sand across the desert. When these grains hit something bigger, they bounce high in the air like acrobats on a circus teeter-

Blowing in the wind

One afternoon in 1898, H. Cecil Booth saw a machine that cleaned trains by blowing the dust away. Booth thought he had a better idea. Instead of blowing dust away, why not suck dust up? He tried out his theory in a restaurant that night. Mr. Booth tried to suck the dust out

of the back of his chair. He nearly choked to death, but it didn't stop his inventive mind.

He dreamed up a machine that sucked dirt through a bag that trapped the dirt but let air pass. His first suction vacuum was the size of

Watch out for dust bunnies

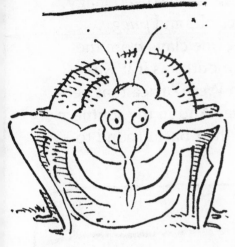

totter. The sand grains spin up to 1000 times per second until they fall back onto the desert. When they land on the tiniest sand grains, those grains go flying in turn. Up to 90 million tonnes (100 million tons) of these tiny sand grains are airborne each year. The hot desert air lifts the sand up to 8 km (5 miles) above sea level. It floats across the world and eventually rains down onto your clothes, your hair, and yes, under your bed.

With all the great dirt in your bed and under your bed, it's not surprising that you've got dirt eaters down there, too. There are more than a million dust mites in an average bed. You can't see them or hear them. But they're everywhere. They look like naked crabs with eight legs. Dust mites don't really eat dust; they eat flakes of skin. And they never go hungry. When you walk, you shed tens of thousands of skin flakes each minute!

THE FIRST VACUUM CLEANER

a fridge and couldn't fit through the door of a house. The next models were so heavy that two people had to operate them.

In spite of the problems, people realized the benefits of sucking dirt up instead of blowing it around. When the soldiers in an army bar-racks started dying of spotted fever, army doctors thought dust in the air was spreading germs. So they called in Booth. After vacuuming, the epidemic ended. The first portable suction vacuum was made in the United States by Hoover in 1908.

EATING DIRT

You won't find it on any menu, but hundreds of millions of people around the world eat dirt every day. Some of you probably eat dirt without even knowing it. Small particles fall into your food. Bits stick to fruits and vegetables. When people deliberately eat dirt, the practice is called geophagy. The word comes from *geo*, meaning earth, and *phagy*, meaning to swallow. Some people dig fine clays from the ground, then pop handfuls into their mouths as if it was popcorn. Dirt-eating is so common in West Africa that people buy dirt pellets in the market-place. And in the southern United States, where dirt-eaters trace their background to Africa, they may bake the clay.

DIRTY DOGS!

Try making these edible clay hot dogs.

You'll need:
1 hot dog per person
aluminum foil
terra-cotta clay
rolling pin
water
oven

1. Wrap each hot dog completely in foil.

2. Flatten a piece of clay with the rolling pin so that it is wide enough and long enough to wrap around your hot dog.

3. Wrap the clay loosely around the hot dog.

4. Seal the hot dog in the clay by wetting the edges of the clay with water and pressing them together.

5. Be creative. You can make a fish, a snake, a prehistoric creature or even a dog, by adding bits of clay and moulding your creature.

6. Bake for 2 hours in a 350°F oven.

7. Admire your creature before cracking it open.

Anthropologists aren't sure why so many people want to eat clay. Perhaps it makes people feel good — some of the African clay is rich in calcium and kaolin, which stops diarrhea. But some clay can make the eaters sick — the clay stops the body from absorbing other needed minerals, such as zinc and iron.

Dirt-eaters are fussy. The taste of clay varies around the world. When dirt-eating Southerners move up North, they don't write home and ask Mom to send them a box of their favourite chocolate chip cookies. Nope, they ask for . . . you guessed it, a box of dirt.

MAKING MUD CAKE

Remember when you were little and liked nothing better than making and serving gucky mud pies? This cake recipe doesn't use real mud, but it gets its name because the cake is dark and chocolatey. It looks difficult to make because of all the ingredients, but it's easy as . . . mud pie. Try it.

You'll need:

an oven
a rectangular cake pan
shortening
a large mixing bowl
an electric beater

150 mL cocoa	⅔ cup
500 mL flour	2 cups
400 mL sugar	1⅔ cup
400 mL water	1⅔ cup
150 mL soft butter	⅔ cup
3 eggs	
10 mL instant coffee	2 tsp.
7 mL baking soda	1½ tsp.
2 mL baking powder	½ tsp.
5 mL vanilla extract	1 tsp.
2 mL salt	½ tsp.

1. Preheat the oven to 350°F.
2. Grease the pan with shortening.
3. Pour all the ingredients into a bowl.
4. Beat everything together for 2 minutes.
5. Pour the mixture into the cake pan.
6. Bake for 40 minutes.

To make the cake really muddy, spread a chocolate fudge icing all over the top and decorate with black licorice.

DIRT FUN

The best games are probably the ones where you end up dirty. Kids around the world have been playing in dirt since the beginning of time. Next time you don't have anything to do . . . go play in the dirt. Here are some ideas to get you started.

Bikers . . . start your pedals!

Whether you call it dirt-bike racing, or BMX — short for bicycle motorcross — it's the fastest growing sport in North America. The trend started in California as a kid version of motorcycle racing. Kids belong to BMX clubs and compete in official races for points and national ranking.

This can be a dangerous sport. The bikes and the bikers have to wear protective clothing. Bikes have thick foam pads covering bars, tubes and sharp edges. Bikers wear official racing helmets, goggles, elbow pads, knee pads, laced-up shoes (slip-on shoes slip off and make you fall) and racing gloves. Head-to-toe clothes are a good idea, too. Bikers race along at speeds of up to 32 km/h (20 mph). If they fall and end in a tangle of legs, spokes, gears, gravel, dirt and mud, they want protection.

Here are some of the main obstacles in a dirt-bike race:

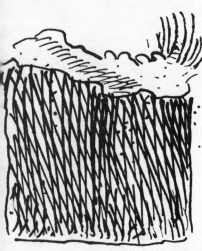

Banzais The most difficult part of a race track. This is a "cliff" as tall as 2 m (6 feet) that riders and their bikes have to go over.

Whoop-de-doo Three bumps in a row. When the bumps are close together, some racers fly over all three as if it was one jump. Sometimes, when the whoop-de-doo is not too steep, racers do a wheelie and ride their back wheel over the bumps. Most racers just take it slowly.

You don't need an official track to have fun with your bikes. Get your friends together and make one in the dirt. Use pails of water and shovels to help you shape the jumps and bumps. When you get bored, try a Slow Bike Race. The object is to ride as slowly as possible without ever touching your feet to the ground. The winner is the slowest rider. Or put cans on the ground so that bikers have to weave in and out and around them.

CHINESE HOP

For this relay race all you need is a patch of dirt, some sticks and some friends — the more the merrier.

1. Divide the players into as many teams as you wish. Each player should find a stick.

2. Lay out the sticks belonging to each team in a ladder-like row. The sticks should be at least 46 cm (18 inches) apart.

3. The teams line up at least 3 m (10 feet) away from their first stick.

4. On the word "Go," the first player on each team runs to the first stick and starts hopping on one foot over each of the sticks. If the player puts two feet down or touches a stick, he or she has to start over.

5. When the player gets to the end of the row of sticks, the player must pick up the last stick and — still hopping — jump back over the sticks to the team to touch the next player in line.

6. The winning team is the team with all the sticks picked up in the least amount of time.

CHAPTER 2

Buried

It's spring. You're helping to put in the garden. The birds are singing. The air is warm. Your shovel hits something hard. Darn, another bone from that dumb dog Fido. Which reminds you of a real groaner. So, you ask your kid sister.

"Hey, Meredith. Did you know Fido has a pedigree?"

"So, where are his papers?"

And you answer, "All over the house." Meredith is not amused. Then your shovel clangs into something else. You dig it up. It looks like a piece of a flower pot. You show it to your parents and they tell you it's probably just junk . . . but check it out anyway.

You'd be amazed at what you can find in your own yard. There might even be the remains of an ancient village. Sound far-fetched? Well, it's not. A team of archaeologists is painstakingly digging up the backyard of a suburban home just outside Toronto because a young boy dug up a piece of pottery. It was a thousand years old. It turns out the boy's find is part of an ancient Indian pottery works. Archaeologists are astonished. Finding any archaeological site in a city is very rare because the evidence is usually destroyed by digging and building.

So keep digging. You might find a fossil, an ancient piece of pottery (called a potsherd), maybe even evidence that an entire village once lived under your carrot patch.

How does stuff from past civilizations get buried? Let's suppose that an ancient Indian settlement once flourished in your backyard. Maybe the people were forced to abandon their homes because of fire, drought or even war. Eventually, the homes rotted and were covered by dirt and then by forests. Hundreds of years pass, then a house-building crew gets to work. They chop down the trees and build your house right on top of the old village. When you dig in the backyard, you find clues about the ancient people who lived on your land.

Over the centuries, people may use the land for different things. The same piece of land could have been the home of Native People, a settlement for pioneers, industrial land and finally, an apartment development with parks. Every time the land is used for something else, the old stuff is built over or covered up.

Archaeologists look for clues to buried civilizations. Mounds of dirt can be a clue that something is buried underneath. Workers at construction sites often unearth artifacts such as ancient tools or bones. Sometimes ancient books refer to cities and places that no longer exist.

Using these clues, archaeologists begin digging. First they divide the area into a grid of small, numbered squares. They carefully dig each square, using small trowels, sometimes even teaspoons and tooth-brushes so they don't break anything valuable. They remove the topsoil — usually about 30 cm (1 foot) deep — and sift it. Any objects they find are labelled and catalogued. Sometimes

23

archaeologists have to coat an item in plaster so that it won't break apart when it is moved.

Each layer of earth reveals secrets from a different time in the past. Archaeologists call these layers "strata." You can see strata in your bedroom when you dig through the piles of clothes and toys in your cupboard. Start at the top of the pile for today's clothes and games. Keep digging and you may reach the clothes and toys you received for last year's birthday buried at the bot-

tom. The deeper down you dig, the farther back in time you go. The same thing happens at an archaeological dig.

Once the objects are found, the archaeologists have to figure out how old they are. They have to piece together bits of pottery and try to remake bowls and cups. Sometimes they try to reconstruct entire buildings and communities from bits and pieces. Archaeologists put our past together like a puzzle with most of the pieces missing.

Underground detectives

In the olden days, when archaeologists were looking for long-buried tombs, they were lucky to stumble on a find. They might circle an area and stick long steel rods into the ground. If they hit metal, it meant something had been found. But what? After a lot of digging, they might discover an empty tomb. Now, archaeologists use machines similar to underground radar to find tombs. Then they dig a hole and lower an upside-down periscope. This allows them to look around and see if the tomb is worth uncovering.

Archaeologists also use airplanes outfitted with cameras to search out new sites. When crops are planted over ruins, they do not grow as tall as other crops. The aerial camera pictures show these "crop marks."

A BURIED CITY

It was August 24, 79 AD, when long-quiet Mount Vesuvius suddenly erupted. Many of the 20 000 people who lived at its foot didn't have time to escape. They were poisoned by the erupting gases and covered in layers of volcanic ash. For several days, the volcano spewed bubbling lava and ash. When it stopped, the towns of Pompeii and Herculaneum were buried under as much as 9 m (30 feet) of mud, ash and lava.

As the years went by, the buried towns were forgotten. Seventeen centuries passed before the Queen of Naples sent her workers on a search for some garden statues. She had heard that a beautiful statue had been found at the foot of Mount Vesuvius.

The queen's workers found statues, then stairs leading down into a theatre. More and more digging over hundreds of years uncovered an entire, perfectly preserved city.

Today if you visit Pompeii, you'll see everything exactly as it was that long-ago August day when Vesuvius erupted. A pig roasts on a fireplace, dogs are tied up at posts and people are huddled in corners with their hands protecting their faces from the deadly fumes. There are even loaves of bread in an oven. The life of a town has been preserved in time.

When the site of Pompeii was first discovered, all of the remains of the people and animals had rotted away. Only holes in the compacted ash showed where they had once been. Then Italian archaeologist Giuseppe Fiorelli had a brilliant idea. He poured plaster into the holes in the lava. When the plaster dried, he had perfect plaster casts of the people. Even the expressions on their faces had been captured. Look at them and you can see how terrifying the volcanic eruption must have been.

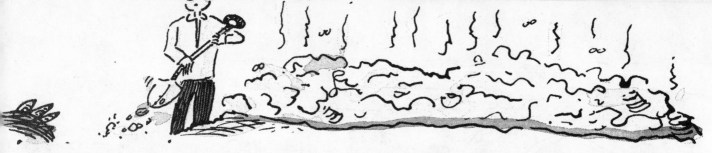

BURYING GARBAGE

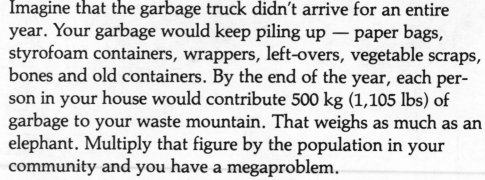

Imagine that the garbage truck didn't arrive for an entire year. Your garbage would keep piling up — paper bags, styrofoam containers, wrappers, left-overs, vegetable scraps, bones and old containers. By the end of the year, each person in your house would contribute 500 kg (1,105 lbs) of garbage to your waste mountain. That weighs as much as an elephant. Multiply that figure by the population in your community and you have a megaproblem.

Garbage has to go somewhere. Most towns truck garbage to vacant land, dump it in huge holes and bury it under dirt. Eventually, this "landfill site" builds into a mountain and is landscaped with trees and grass. Some towns even turn old landfill sites into ski hills in winter.

There are problems with landfill sites. People throw hazardous household waste into the trash without even realizing they may be poisoning the environment. When bleach mixes with ammonia, there can be an explosion, and deadly gases can be created. Medicines, pesticides and oven cleaners can be lethal. Chemicals can seep into water flowing deep underground and poison wells and water supplies. And besides the dangers of burying waste, the world is running out of landfill sites.

It's not all glum news. You can help by recycling paper, plastics and tins. Better yet, stop using as much paper and reuse your plastic bags. Start a compost heap (see page 39). Everyone has to do something to cut down on garbage. Industry is swapping wastes — what one company might throw out, another could use as a raw material. And more communities are starting curbside recycling programs.

BURIED TREASURE!

There's a booby-trapped shaft, called the Money Pit, on Oak Island, Nova Scotia. Some folks think there's a buried treasure there, but there's no way of knowing. People have spent millions of dollars trying to get to the treasure. Whenever someone gets close to the bottom of the pit, things go wrong. Six men have died trying. Some of them smothered in cave-ins; others drowned when the shaft flooded with sea water.

The saga of the Oak Island Mystery began in 1795 when a Nova Scotia farm boy named Daniel McGinnis found a clearing in the middle of a red oak forest. There'd been rumours for years that pirates used to land on Oak Island and hide their bounty. And so, when Daniel saw a clearing smack in the middle of the dense forest and then noticed a patch of sunken land and some odd carvings on a tree trunk, he was sure he'd stumbled on the place where the treasure was buried.

29

He raced to find friends and they started digging. They eased up a layer of stones and found themselves staring into a shallow shaft. There was only one reason for it to be there — someone had buried something.

They climbed in and kept digging. They hit a platform of rotted logs. They broke it apart and continued digging. Whenever they thought they'd struck gold — wham! — they'd hit wood. Every 3 m (10 feet), it was the same thing.

At 27 m (90 feet) down, there was a layer of charcoal, putty and coconut fibre. What was a coconut doing down a shaft? Then their shovels hit rock. They brushed away the dirt and discovered a stone. It was etched with odd symbols. It wasn't a language. Could it have been a secret code? They pried up the stone and suddenly, water started pouring into the shaft. Just as they scrambled out to safety, they poked with the end of their shovel and felt something hard — like a chest — a bit farther down. But they never reached it. By morning, the shaft was full of sea water.

Nobody could figure out how to drain the shaft, so the Money Pit lay untouched for another 46 years. New fortune hunters came along and used a drill. It pulled up small pieces of metal. Still, not a dubloon or a ruby was found. But the mystery of the flooding shaft was solved. Whoever dug the shaft booby-trapped it by digging two flood tunnels from the shaft to the ocean. At high tide, the water pours in at 4500 L (1000 gallons) a minute! The tricks didn't stop there — the crafty pirates probably dug tunnels that sloped gently upwards from the main shaft. The treasure might be hidden in them. One thing is clear — somebody went to a lot of trouble to hide something.

There have been enough clues to keep treasure hunters pouring their fortunes into the fortune-hunting. They have

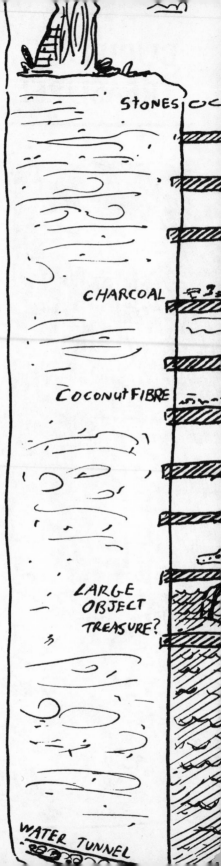

LOG PLATFORM ONE EVERY 3M.

Putty

Stone with Symbols

Water Tunnel

dug up china, brass, a pair of 300-year-old Spanish scissors and an ancient chunk of wood.

There have been so many digs that the original Money Pit has caved in. One company has spent more than $10 million and has still come up with nothing. But that won't stop them. Folks are convinced the treasure is Bluebeard's Bounty, Inca gold or the crown jewels of France. But for now, the mystery of Oak Island remains buried at the bottom of the Money Pit.

Buried alive

The African lungfish usually lives in the muddy bottoms of swamps and lakes. It snuggles in the soft mud and comes up to the surface for air. During droughts, the lungfish folds up its 2-m (6-foot) long body, coats itself with mucus and goes into a deep sleep called estivation (hibernation during the hot season). Without water, the mud around the lungfish bakes into a hard shell. Amazingly, the lungfish can exist inside this mud coffin without food and water for four years. When the rains start, the mud softens and the lungfish comes out of estivation.

BURIAL PRACTICES

Why do dogs bury bones? So that other dogs and animals won't find them. And maybe because the meat on the buried bone decays more slowly thanks to the cooler temperatures underground. Burying a bone is like putting it in the refrigerator.

Dogs aren't the only creatures who bury things . . . .

A buried army

In 1974, archaeologists unearthed an entire Chinese army. They were digging on a peasant's farm when they uncovered plaster, woven mats and wooden beams. They thought they'd found a palace. Actually, they had uncovered the tomb of the first emperor of China, who died in 210 BC. There were 7000 clay soldiers standing in long corridors and rooms guarding their emperor into the "next life."

The clay army was magnificent. Each statue was life-sized, hollow and beautifully carved. The expressions on the statues' faces were all different. They wore full costumes and carried weapons. They were accompanied by clay horses and chariots.

Buried above ground

Ancient people around the world once buried people and chariots and even treasure ships under mounds of dirt. In Japan, the Emperor Nintoku is buried in a mound that took 20 years to build and is surrounded by three moats. The prehistoric Adena and Hopewell Indians of the eastern United States buried their dead in cone-shaped mounds filled with jewels and gold. Sometime between 1000 BC and 1700 AD, the effigy mound culture Indians shaped giant mounds to look like beasts and birds. You can still see a giant serpent mound they built in Ohio that winds more than 400 m (1300 feet). The dead were buried in the head or heart of the animal mound.

My mummy, the mummy

When the Egyptians made mummies, they removed the body organs that decompose most quickly — the stomach, intestines, lungs and liver. The heart was always left in the body since it was considered the place of understanding. Don't ask about the brain — you don't want to know. (Brave souls can turn to page 78.)

Each of the organs was placed in a separate burial jar that was sealed with stoppers and decorated with a human or animal head for protection. A jackal protected the stomach, a falcon protected the intestines, an ape protected the lungs and a human guarded the liver. These four jars were always buried with the body.

MUD-DLING THROUGH

Mud is more than a gushy mushy mixture of soil and water that makes gloopy sounds when you walk in it. It serves a useful purpose — it helps to preserve plants and animals that lived millions of years ago. A plant or animal becomes buried in mud. As the mud hardens and time passes, a fossil forms.

Fossils are like people — they come in all shapes and sizes. All fossils, however, are the preserved remains of plants and animals. Sometimes, but

Old-time insect

The oldest fossilized insect in the world was found embedded in mud-stone on the north shore of the Gaspé in Quebec. It is a relative of the pesky silver-fish. Its birthday? Three hundred and ninety million years ago.

rarely, the entire animal, skin, teeth and bones, gets fossilized. Whole ancient animals have been found in hardened mud and tar pits, but more often only parts of the plant or animal are fossilized.

Here's what happens. When the plant or animal dies, it is buried in sand or mud. The soft parts rot, leaving only the shells or bone. Water flows in and around the left-over bits and seeps into tiny holes in shell or bone. When the water dries up, minerals are left behind. These minerals change the shell or bone into rock.

Fossils are everywhere . . . but you have to keep your eyes open. The next time you walk along a rocky shore, pick up the rocks and look at them closely. Or look along roadside rocks that have been blasted to make way for a highway. If you are lucky, you may even find fossils of dinosaur footprints from millions of years ago.

Future fossil hot spots

Where will future fossil hunters find fossils being formed today? River deltas are a likely place because the sediment left there will eventually harden into rock and imprison skeletons from today. Close to active volcanoes is another good spot. Imagine what lies under the ash of Mount St. Helens!

35

MUDDY FOOT PRINTS

Imagine creatures walking through a prehistoric forest. They lumber along a muddy river edge and stop for a drink. And then a rain of volcanic ash covers the forest and fills the footprints. Eventually, the mud hardens into rock. For a million years the footprints are buried under volcanic ash. When they're discovered, the footprints give scientists information about the size and habits of the creatures who made them. Scientists call these "trace fossils" because they preserve traces of animals who lived long ago. Here's how you can preserve your own muddy footprints.

You'll need:

a *muddy place on a dry day*
    (your trace fossil has to dry fast!)
tape
a *long strip of cardboard*
water
plaster of Paris
an old tin can
a *stick*

1. Step into the mud and walk until you've got a clear footprint.

2. Tape the edges of the cardboard together so you have an oval large enough to circle your footprint.

3. Press this cardboard collar into the mud around your print.

4. Mix the water and plaster of Paris in the tin can until it is as thick as pancake batter.

5. Pour the wet plaster of Paris into your cardboard collar. It should be about 2.5 cm (1 inch) thick.

6. Let it dry. This takes about half a day.

7. Lift the cardboard and plaster cast. Carefully wipe away any dirt.

You can also look for animal tracks and make plaster casts of them too.

MY FOOT

CHAPTER 3

The Dirt on Dirt

Take a good look at a handful of dirt. Feel it, smell it, crumble it between your fingers. What do you discover? If you sample dirt from different places, you'll see that each handful is a little different. One handful might feel hard but squish into slimy paste between your fingers; another sample may almost float away in the air because it is so dry.

Dirt is both organic (made of things that are living, or were once living) and inorganic (made of things that have never lived, such as crushed rock). How a handful looks and feels depends on the type of plants and animals around, the kind of weather and the kind of rocks under the soil.

Have you ever seen red or yellow soil? How about blue, brown or black soil? It's there if you look for it. When dirt looks red, there is some iron in the local rocks. When dirt is grey or even blue, it means there is marshland. If you grab a handful of dirt that is deep brown or black . . . start growing. You have found terrific growing soil, rich in humus. Humus is the main ingredient in rich topsoil. It's made from nature's garbage — rotted leaves, sticks, roots and dead insects — and nature's living recyclers — fungi, mold, bacteria and earthworms.

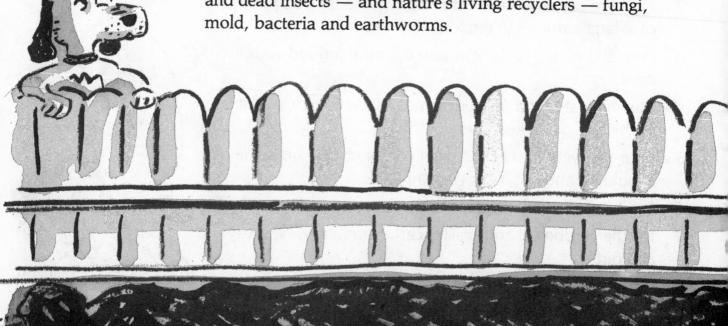

DIRT — MAKE THE BEST PART YOURSELF

Gardeners know that the biggest, healthiest plants grow when they add humus to the topsoil. Humus is just rotted leaves, grasses and vegetable scraps. You can make your own humus by starting a compost heap.

The combination of heat, water, bacteria and garbage makes a nutritious mix for your garden. Don't worry that your compost heap will stink. If you follow the directions, there'll be no smell at all.

You'll need:
a *shovel*
soil
an *old wooden box with slats*
household garbage — vegetable peelings, grass clippings, leaves, paper — no grease or meat
water

1. Shovel a layer of soil into the container.
2. Throw in a layer of garbage including some grass clippings, leaves, vegetable peelings and water.
3. Cover the garbage with another layer of soil and mix together.
4. Keep your composter outside where the rain will keep it moist.
5. Keep adding garbage and soil and stir it around.
6. In about two months, you'll have dark, goopy stuff. This is humus. Feed it to your garden . . . and it will thank you.

WOODEN BOX

SOIL

GARBAGE - GRASS, LEAVES VEGETABLE PEELS - WATER

SOIL

SILT, SAND, ETC.

Put a handful of dirt into a jar, fill it with water, give it a good shake and leave it around for awhile. Take a look at what you've got. The dirt settles into layers. The water looks muddy because really fine pieces of dirt are floating in the water. Pour the water through a paper coffee filter and see what you find.

Humus: This dark, moist layer is made when food, leaves, sticks, roots and insects die and rot.

Clay: This slimy, slippery goop is made up of particles that are smaller than 0.004 mm (0.00016 in).

Silt: Mud formed from tiny pieces of rock makes up silt. Its fine grains measure from 0.004 (0.00016 in) mm to 0.06 mm (0.0024 in).

Sand: These coarse grains measure from 0.06 mm (0.0024 in) to 2.0 mm (0.08 in).

Gravel: Larger, visible rock particles are called gravel.

- HUMUS
- CLAY
- SILT
- SAND
- GRAVEL

Tired of sand-coloured sand?

Sand can be almost any colour. The coral-coloured sand of Bermuda is made of limestone, coral and shell fragments. The black sands of Hawaii were made from molten rock of volcanoes that cooled and was washed to the sea by mountain streams. There is even green sand on the ocean floor — it contains bits of glauconite.

The granddaddy of rocks

Some Australian university students discovered the world's oldest rocks. They contain tiny crystals of zircon sandwiched in sandstone and they're 4.2 billion years old!

HOW ROCKS BECOME DIRT

As you read these words, rocks around the world are slowly changing into dirt. This process is called weathering and you can see signs of it at work all around you.

Sculpted rocks

When you see rocks that look like this, you know that wind or water have been at work. They rub off bits of rock that eventually become dirt. One famous Canadian landmark, Percé Rock in Quebec, has a hole 30 m (100 feet) wide carved through it by waves crashing against it. The Grand Canyon was carved by rushing waters.

Pebbles

Visit a pebble beach and you're seeing rocks on their way to becoming sand, an important ingredient in dirt. Large rocks are tumbled like clothes in a dryer until they break apart and all the rough edges get worn off.

Cracks in rocks

The sun warms up rocks during the day. The rocks get bigger. But at night, when the temperature drops, the rocks shrink. Eventually, the rocks crack. When water gets into the cracks and freezes, it makes the cracks even bigger. Bits of rock fall off and are worn down even more by wind and rain.

Plants start to grow in small crevices in the rock and force bits of the rock to crumble off. These tiny bits become the dirt in which other plants grow.

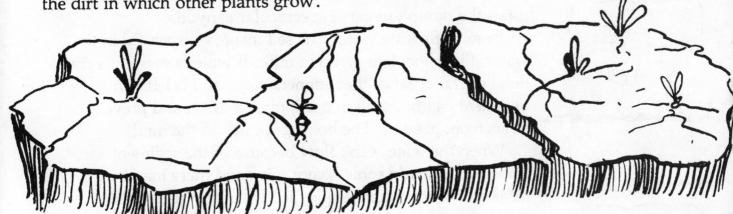

On the rocks

Some of the dirt in your backyard was probably made by glaciers millions of years ago. Glaciers are thick slabs of ice that long ago crushed or gouged rocks in their path. Wind and water wore the rocks down even more. Soon, microscopic bacteria and plants started to live and die between the rock crevices and among the pebbles. It can take anywhere from 100 years to 10 000 years to make 2 cm (⅝ inch) of good topsoil from crushed rock.

43

DISAPPEAR-ING DIRT

Dirt on the move is called erosion. Erosion changes the way our world looks. Sometimes the results are awesome sculptures — Niagara Falls and the Grand Canyon were both caused by rivers eroding rock. Sometimes erosion is deadly. It can cause rock slides, mud slides and floods.

Water causes erosion. Rivers moving through rock or flat land carve a path and remove loose rock and soil called sediment. The amount of erosion depends on the volume of water and how fast it moves. A slow trickle of water on the prairies will gradually eat away the land, but there's no way it has the oomph to carve spectacular canyons.

In swift-flowing water, the sediment is suspended in the water, like chocolate syrup in milk. If water slows for a river bend or flatter land, the sediment sinks and is left behind. Sediment can build up in a shipping channel and prevent boats from passing. The boats get stuck in the mud.

When the water can't flow because of the sediment, floods occur. Add some heavy rains and there may be a disaster. Nine million people died when the Yellow River flooded in China during the last century.

Heavy rains can turn dry, loose soil into mud slides, destroying homes and lives.

Wind is another cause of erosion. It lifts dry soil into the air. Your grandparents might remember the incredible dust storms of the 1930s. They stripped farms of good growing soil and led to ten long years of drought called the "Dirty Thirties."

During those years, the wind blew black clouds of dirt 8 km (5 miles) high around the prairies and even out to sea. Drifts of sand and silt buried homes and barns. No crops grew.

Nature can't take all the blame for the bad things caused by erosion. People have abused the land and allowed erosion

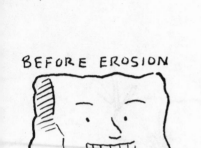

BEFORE EROSION

to wreak havoc. Land that was once fertile is now desert because settlers cut the trees for homes and fuel. Their animals grazed on what remained of the plants. With nothing to anchor the topsoil, it blew away or was washed away. Only drifting dust and sand was left. Deserts are growing across North America and Africa. The Sahara Desert is growing by 78 km² (30 square miles) a year.

It might not be too late to save the disappearing land. River erosion can be stopped by building special barriers called jetties to catch and trap sediment. Trees, shrubs and grasses can be planted on farm fields to anchor the sand and soil. Crops can be irrigated so that their roots grow deep and hold down the soil. And ploughing can be done in ways that hold the soil instead of letting it run off with the rain. How? Turn the page to find out.

AFTER EROSION

Oops, there goes another sycamore tree

Sometimes it's too late to do anything about erosion. Ask Mrs. Mae Rose Owen of Winter Park, Florida. In 1981, Mrs. Owen called police. Her giant sycamore tree had been swallowed into the earth, she reported. Soon there were more calls to the police. Half of a swimming pool had sunk into the ground; a whole section of the street disappeared. What was going on? Before the mystery was solved, there was a sink-hole in the middle of Winter Park, 45 m (150 feet) deep and 120 m (400 feet) wide.

Over millions of years, water had eroded the limestone rock under Winter Park, creating an enormous cavern. Usually, the cavern was flooded with water. But there had been a drought and the water level was low. It couldn't support the top-soil — or the town — any more. earth started to sink and dragged parts of the town down with it, including Mrs. Owen's sycamore.

MESSY FARMS

Farmers compete in ploughing contests — the winner is the farmer who ploughs the neatest, straightest rows. It used to be that all farmers took pride in this kind of ploughing. They would plough the old crops under and make neat, straight furrows for seeding. That's changing because the old way is probably not the best way.

On hilly land, the neat, ploughed fields get washed away by rain. When old crops are churned into the ground by the

You'll need:
2 cookie sheets
potting soil or topsoil
sprinkler (or rainy day)

It's easier to do this project outside.

super-powerful new ploughs, the old leaves and roots are buried so deeply they cannot decompose and add nutrients to the soil. So farmers are going the messy route. Some of them don't plough at all. They leave the old plants to decay naturally and sow their seeds in and around the debris. Others still plough, but instead of making straight rows, they contour plough. The farmer moves across the field and makes one long unbroken coil. You can see why this works.

1. Make two "fields" by mounding the dirt on the cookie sheets. Make each "field" a hill by putting more dirt at one end of the cookie sheets.

2. Run your finger through one "field" and plough in straight rows. On the other field do contour ploughing.

3 Angle each cookie sheet slightly so the field is on a bit of a slope. (Try supporting one end of the cookie sheet on a bottom step.)

4. Water lightly with sprinkler.

5. Watch to see which field loses the most soil.

The results of messy fields? Good crops from rich fields.

HERE'S MUD IN YOUR EYE

Go outside on a windy day and you're almost sure to find yourself blinking hard. You can't see them, but tiny specks of dirt are everywhere in the air. And — ouch — a big one has just landed in your eye.

Small particles of dirt, smaller than the dust under your bed, are important. Without them there wouldn't be any rain. Water in the air must have something to stick onto to grow into raindrops. And beautiful sunsets would be impossible without dirt.

The sun's light is made up of all the colours of the rainbow. The colours are different wavelengths. Red has the longest wavelength; violet has the shortest. At the end of the day when the sun is near the horizon, its light must pass through the low layer of dust and air near the earth.

The short wavelength colours such as blue and violet bounce off the dust particles to give a dusky glow to the sky. The longer wavelength colours such as red come through the dust. This makes the sun look a brilliant red.

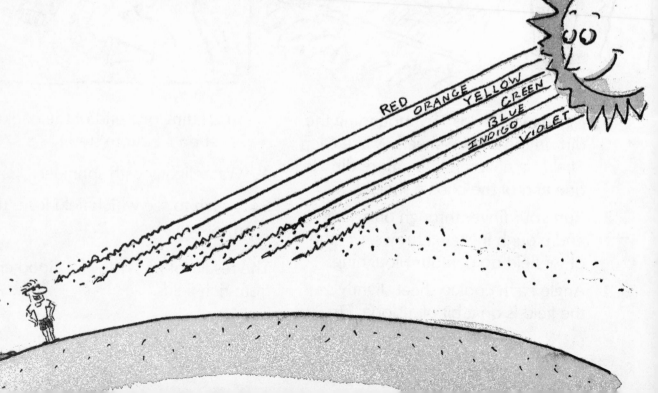

Sometimes dirt really gets moving in the air. Imagine sitting on the porch on a calm, hot afternoon under clear skies. In the distance you see a column of dust 300 m (1000 feet) high, swirling rapidly over the land and picking up dust, straw and leaves. You've just seen a dust devil. They rarely cause large-scale damage and usually happen in desert areas. When a flat, bare patch of earth gets overheated, a current of warm air starts to rise. Air flows in from all directions to equalize the pressure. The air swirls upward in a spiral.

Quicksand!

The land beneath your feet is always shifting. You may think the shiftiest sand, quicksand, is imaginary stuff of adventure movies. Think again — quicksand is very real and exists across North America.

Dry sand sticks together. Wet sand becomes fluid, like water. If pressure builds under really wet sand — let's say from an underground stream — it becomes quicksand.

People die in quicksand when they panic and thrash around. If you move quickly in quicksand, it loosens for an instant and then packs even more tightly around you. But you can float on quicksand by lying back and gently moving your arms. Then you can backstroke until you're on solid ground.

Sand sculpture — nature's way

Think before you scramble up an enormous sand dune the next time you're at the shore. The dunes look solid, but they are so fragile that a single footprint could start their collapse.

Dunes get their start when strong currents and high winds deposit sand from the lake or ocean floor onto the beach. The wind picks up the sand and carries it until the sand hits an obstacle, such as a piece of driftwood or grass. The sand starts to build up. Grass grows and spreads anchoring roots under the surface. When dunes get really high, wind storms, rain or even people walking can destroy the grass root anchors. That frees the sand to blow farther inland. The sand can pile up against forests and bury them.

That's why you'll find sand fences to trap the sand and walkways at protected beaches.

MAKE YOUR OWN SAND SCULPTURE

You'll need:
damp sand
water
imagination

Don't stop with sand castles. Make life-sized whales, mermaids, dinosaurs, birds . . . anything! Draw your design onto damp sand. Start packing sand into the design. Keep your sand wet to create depressions and built-up areas. You can make your sculpture really special by adding shells, seaweed, driftwood and other beach finds. Try draping seaweed hair to cover a modest mermaid and cover the tail with seashells. Once you've finished, see if you can come up with a way to protect your sand sculpture from being blown away by the wind or washed away by the water. Will a fence help? A moat?

If you can't bear to see your sand sculpture disappear with the tide, try making sand-clay.

You'll need:
a spoon
saucepan
500 mL sand   *(2 cups)*
250 mL cornstarch (1 cup)
250 mL water   *(1 cup)*

1. Mix the sand, cornstarch and water together in a pan.

2. Heat the mixture over low heat. Keep stirring.

3. Remove from heat when the mixture is thick.

4. Let the mixture cool, then make your sculpture.

5. Let your sculpture dry and harden.

DIRT ON THE MOVE

Suppose someone said to you, "Jason is solid as a rock," or, "Lee has her feet firmly planted on the ground." You'd probably think that Jason and Lee were pretty dependable people. After all, the ground is always solid and steady beneath your feet. Or is it? You may be surprised to learn that rocks are constantly crumbling and the ground is slowly shifting. Without all this movement, there wouldn't be any dirt. Nor would there be any mountains, caverns, canyons or gorges. What a flat, dull, place our world would be.

We live on the earth's crust, but it's not a solid piece of rock. It's made up of seven huge slabs, called "plates," that float like icebergs on the surface. These plates are constantly moving, sliding over and under and even bashing into each other like giant water bumper cars.

Usually the plates move slowly, about 2.5 cm to 5 cm (1 to 2 inches) a year. When two plates move away from each other, they leave a gap between them. Hot liquid rock called magma from inside the earth oozes out through the gap. Huge chains of volcanoes may form in this way, often on the

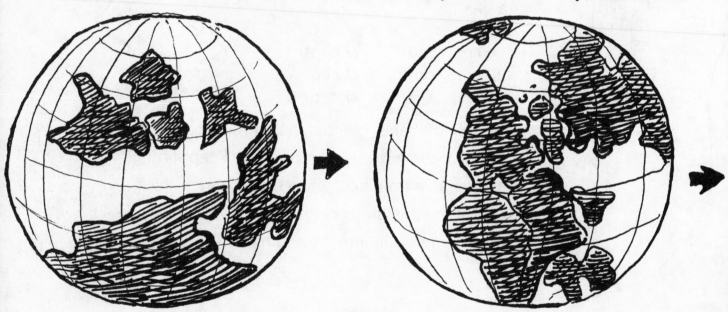

400 MILLION YEARS AGO   150 MILLION YEARS AGO

ocean floor. Some of these underwater mountains grow until they poke out through the surface of the water, forming an island. Iceland is one such island.

Sometimes two plates scrape together and one gets snagged on the other. When this happens, enormous pressure builds up until, finally, an earthquake releases some of the pressure.

Plates can also push up against each other, folding the land upward into mountains. That's usually a slow process. The Himalayan mountains started to grow 25 million years ago and are still growing taller because the plate on which India sits is playing push-shove with the Eurasian plate.

This up-thrusting can lift land from the bottom of the sea to the tops of mountains. Mountain climbers at the top of Mount Everest discovered limestone. It's made from crushed sea shells usually found on the ocean floor. These rock clues tell geologists where the land that is now mountains first came from.

No, this isn't a jigsaw puzzle. This is how the continents look today and how they looked in the past. The plates on which the continents sit keep shifting.

8 MILLION YEARS AGO   TODAY

DIGGING DOWN DEEP

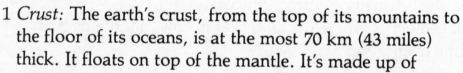

Ever try digging to the centre of the earth? How far did you get? Probably not very far. You're not alone. Even geologists with sophisticated equipment have never dug into the earth's mantle.

The deepest hole so far took 20 years to drill and pierces only 12 km (7.5 miles) into the earth. But even it doesn't break through the earth's crust. What's the big problem with deep digging? First, there is no torque (twisting force) when you drill with such a long drill. One geologist says it is "like drilling with a piece of spaghetti." Second, it gets hotter as you dig deeper — so hot that the drill starts to melt!

So forget about drilling to the centre of the earth. But if you could slice through the earth much as you slice through an apple, here's what you'd see:

1 *Crust:* The earth's crust, from the top of its mountains to the floor of its oceans, is at the most 70 km (43 miles) thick. It floats on top of the mantle. It's made up of
   • Topsoil: It takes years to make just 2.5 cm (1 inch) of topsoil.
   • Subsoil: This is made up of mineral particles.
   • Bedrock: This is where oil and gas are found.

2 *Mantle:* The top layer of the mantle is hot rock, some of which is a hot liquid called magma. When magma erupts through a volcano, it's called lava.

3 *Core:* The liquid Outer Core and solid Inner Core are made mainly of iron and some nickel, silicon and sulphur. Geologists think the temperature at the centre of the earth is 6000° C (10 800° F).

CRUST

MANTLE

OUTER CORE

INNER CORE

T-E-R-R-A-N-E

T-E-R-R-A-I-N

That's t-e-r-r-a-n-e

Spelling buffs may want to correct a geologist who writes about the earth's terrane. Shouldn't that be terrain? Nope, they are two different things. Terrain is how the land looks — whether it has mountains, lakes or swamp land. Terrane is a new word that means a block of the earth's crust.

Geologists in British Columbia discovered fossils of sea creatures that lived 250 million years ago in Asia. How did Asian fossils get to Canada? It seems that 200 million years ago, an enormous terrane, or supercontinent, in the South Pacific broke apart. The pieces travelled all along the North American coast leaving traces behind.

CHAPTER 4

Dirt Homes

There is another world under your feet that is home to many animals. Moles tunnel, owls burrow, ants excavate, earthworms devour and brown rats race in underground mazes. Ready to take a peek under your feet and see what lurks below?

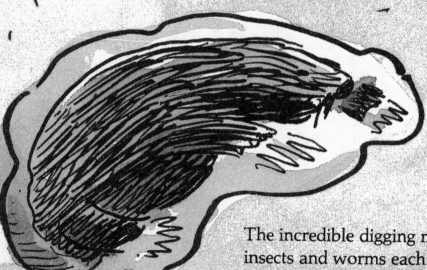

Charles Darwin used to play music to his worms. They ate during high notes and scurried underground on low notes. What do you think they'd do to heavy metal? For more about the amazing earthworm, turn the page.

The incredible digging mole can eat 40 000 insects and worms each year.

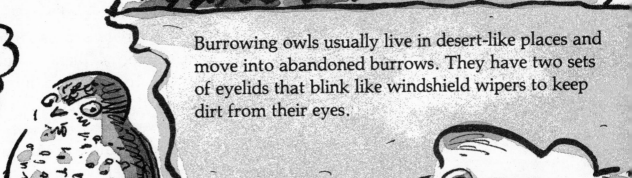

Burrowing owls usually live in desert-like places and move into abandoned burrows. They have two sets of eyelids that blink like windshield wipers to keep dirt from their eyes.

Brown Rats really are smart. Once they discover poison bait, they stay away . . . even if it's disguised or moved about. They scurry under the cover of dirt, leaves or snow to avoid predators such as cats and birds.

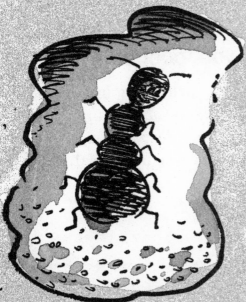

Some ants have "ant cows." These are really aphids, little insects that suck the juice out of plants to make sugar water. The ants protect the aphids and even tend their eggs underground. What do the ants get out of it? You guessed it — a sweet drink they "milk" from their "cows."

57

PLANT'S BEST FRIEND

Your garden would be a disaster without earthworms. They turn rotting plants and animals into rich fertilizer. And, as they burrow through the soil, they create spaces for air and water to penetrate. Without earthworms, plants would have a tough time. Surprised? Take this True or False quiz and find out about some surprising earthworm facts. Answers on page 78.

1. Earthworms are both male and female and can have babies without ever meeting another worm.
2. Earthworms breathe through special holes near their tails.
3. A single hectare of land can be home to 23 000 earthworms. (A single acre is home to 56 800 earthworms.)

There are two of these little legs called setae on each segment. They help the worm move and allow it to cling to the sides of the burrow as it inches out to feed.

Worms have as many as 200 of these segments.

Earthwooooooooorm!

The longest earthworm in the world measured 6.7 m (22 feet) and was found in South Africa. Imagine how a robin would feel if it met this monster!

4. If you cut an earthworm in half, it will grow a new head or a new tail.
5. Earthworms hibernate in the winter.
6. Some earthworms grow to be 3.6 m (12 feet) long, weigh 0.6 kg (1½ pounds) and make gurgling noises when they move.
7. People once believed that earthworms fell from the sky when it rained.
8. Earthworms eat their weight in soil every day.
9. An earthworm is tough to pull out of its burrow because it glues itself to the soil.

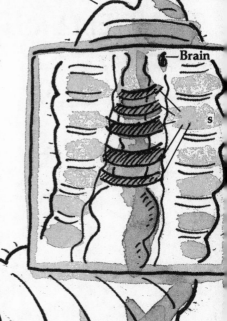

The mouth looks like a shovel and is called the prostomium. It sweeps the ground.

Brain

S

Sneak up on a worm

Worms come out at night, but they disappear if you go close to them with a flashlight. Try covering your light with red cellophane — worms can't see red light! Walk softly — worms feel vibrations and will retreat into their burrows.

MOLE TUNNELLERS

Earthworms know who to watch out for underground — moles. Moles are superbly adapted for what they do — eat and dig!

Moles have to eat frequently; they have no stomach in which to store food. Every four hours, moles take a snack break. They eat earthworms, spiders, grubs, centipedes and insects. Moles are super-sensitive to movement; they can sense an insect that is moving through a tunnel far away. Insects beware!

When a mole digs a burrow, it claws the soil loose and pushes it up towards the surface. Then it tucks its snout between its legs and spins around. The rotary action makes a neat pile on the ground. This is the molehill entrance to the burrow.

When digging, the mole scoops dirt with its forefeet, shoves loose dirt under its body and kicks it back with its hind feet. Every so often the mole faces the other way, braces itself against the tunnel walls with one forefoot and shoves the dirt back up through the tunnel with the palm of its other foot. The hind feet keep kicking to move the mole up and forward.

The mole's nest is at the bottom of the entrance tunnel. It's the first thing the mole digs. Next comes an escape tunnel and tunnels for finding food. As the mole rubs against the tunnel walls, they become smooth. That way there are no rough patches to slow it down when it's hunting for food.

A mole can tunnel up to 4.5 m (15 feet) an hour. A tunnel 23 m (75 feet) long is just one night's work.

A mole's fur is short and smooth — it helps the mole glide through the dirt.

Strong shoulders and limbs are good for heavy-duty digging.

Its paws are at right angles to the arm for easier digging.

Its ears are small so that dirt doesn't get into them.

MACHINE TUNNELLERS

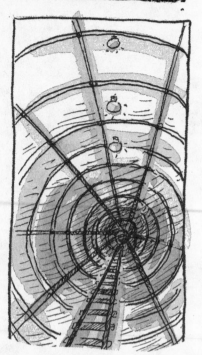

When people build tunnels, they must do a lot more planning than the mole does. Engineers design the tunnels. Geologists dig into the soil and rock to take samples and decide the best places and the best ways to dig. Then the digging begins.

Workers dig a shaft into the ground. All of the equipment and men enter the tunnel through this shaft. Two crews of tunnel builders dig in opposite directions to speed up the work.

Bulldozers and shovels are used to dig out the mud. Often, large tunnels are "shield driven." This means a large circular piece of metal is shoved through the ground by hydraulic jacks. Little railway cars are loaded with the rocks and debris that must be removed from the tunnel.

Workers support the sides and top of the tunnel with pieces of curved steel called ribs. Sometimes, the tunnel is coated in a layer of concrete or long bolts are drilled through the tunnel roof and held firmly to the surrounding rock. This prevents tunnel cave-ins.

Tunnel trivia

The longest rail tunnel in the world is the Seikan Rail Tunnel under the Tsugaru Strait between two Japanese islands of Honshu and Hokkai. The tunnel is 54 km (33 miles) long and took 20 years and 10 months to finish. Thirty-four workers died building the tunnel that is 240 m (787 feet) below sea level.

The longest continuous subway tunnel is in Moscow. It runs for 30.7 km (19.07 miles).

The tunnel with the biggest diameter — 23 m (76 feet) wide and 17 m (58 feet) high — is in Yerba Buena Island, San Francisco. More than 80 million cars, trucks and buses move through this two-level tunnel every year.

Watch out beloooooooooowww

The Tower of Pisa in Italy leans a little farther to one side every year. Architects think it may topple over one day.

The probable reason is that the builders in 1174 didn't know much about dirt. The builders made the foundations for the tower the same size as the tower. Unfortunately, they built the tower on sandy soil that was softer on one side than the other. The tower started to sink lower and lower on the soft side!

Builders today would bore into the soil at different depths and in different places, then study the samples to decide how much weight the soil could hold. Rock, clay and sand support different weights. They might build a wide foundation to spread the weight of a tower. Or, they might decide that the ground could not support a tall building. They would sink posts made of concrete and steel, called piles, into the ground and build on top of them.

DIRT ABOVE GROUND

When people around the world make homes for themselves, they look for materials that are cheap and handy. You can't get much cheaper than mud.

Building with dirt is an idea people have borrowed from animals. Termites in Africa dot the flatlands with volcano-shaped mud homes like the ones you see above, on the left. Some mounds are as tall as barns. Some birds use mud to cement twigs and leaves together for sturdy nests, and beavers pack their dams with mud for waterproofing and weatherproofing.

Keeping warm in winter and cool in summer leads some people to dig right into the sides of hills to make their homes. The earth helps insulate the house. Other people shovel a layer of dirt onto their roofs and plant grass on it. Grass is a good roofing material — it keeps out the rain and keeps the inside temperature even. How do these homeowners keep the roof from growing? Why, they get a goat, of course.

Africans and Native People from the southern United States and Central America use dirt for building. They mix mud with grass and straw. This material, called adobe, can be spread over a twig frame while it's still wet or can be patted into shapes and baked in the sun until it's hard. Adobe homes more than 10 000 years old have been discovered in the Middle East.

Today we use a modern version of adobe — bricks. A brick house is weathertight and impervious to rain and snow. And, no matter how hard the big bad wolf huffs and puffs, he's out of luck.

INSIDE A
BRICKWORKS

SHALE

1 Shale (a hardened clay that splinters when it's taken out of the ground) is crushed to a fine powder between grinding wheels.

2 The powdered shale is mixed with water in a machine called a pug mill until it looks and feels just right. (You can squeeze it between your fingers but no water drips out.)

3 Under high pressure, the clay is pushed like toothpaste through a tube. A rectangular form gives the clay square corners. Metal rods inside the tube make holes in the clay. The shaped clay is called a slug.

4 Wires cut the slugs into bricks which are loaded onto railway-type cars and dried in an oven at 200°C (400°F) for 60 hours. The bricks are dried slowly so they don't crack.

5 The bricks are "fired." They move slowly through a kiln. The temperature inside the kiln gradually increases from 200°C (400°F) to more than 1000°C (1900°F). This takes another 60 hours.

6 Cool air is blown on the bricks to cool them down. Then the bricks are stacked on top of each other until they make a huge cube of 500 bricks. They are lifted onto trucks for delivery.

MAKE YOUR OWN BRICKS

All the ingredients for making bricks are right in your own backyard.

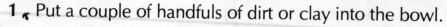

You'll need:
a large bowl
dirt or clay
water
grass clippings or small pieces of straw
scissors
an empty 1-L (1-quart) milk carton
Vaseline
a large spoon

1. Put a couple of handfuls of dirt or clay into the bowl.

2. Add water until your goop looks like pancake batter.

3. Add grass and straw to bind the dirt together.

4. Cut the milk carton lengthwise to make a brick mould.

5. Grease the mould with Vaseline.

6. Spoon the wet mud into the mould until it is full. Make sure it's even by thumping the mould on a table a few times.

7. Put the mould in the sun to dry. It will take a few hot, dry days to bake.

If you and your friends make enough bricks, you can build an adobe clubhouse. Do it outside. Stack the bricks and use mud to stick the bricks together. If you want to be really fancy, smooth a layer of mud over the entire clubhouse once it's made, for a professional finish.

Another good idea: If you save milk cartons, you can make "fake" brick houses. Take the tops off the cartons. Stuff one carton with newspapers. Slide it inside an empty carton, open end first. You have a building brick that will hold up. Stick the bricks together with masking tape or heavy-duty glue. Children in Boston built a library inside a museum this way!

CHAPTER 5

Dirt for GARDENING

Have you ever eaten a tomato picked straight off the vine or chased a butterfly through a meadow? That's only for country kids, right? No way. If you have dirt, you can have wild gardens or neat, tended pots of veggies . . . anywhere.

City slickers can be downtown farmers. Downtown spaces are being turned into beautiful, wild parkland. Even balconies and roof-tops can be made into flower and vegetable gardens.

Some schools are turning concrete playgrounds into natural meadows so kids can smell the flowers and watch the butterflies. Can you imagine building ponds and planting vines in your school yard? It's being done. Some schools have their own nature preserves for ducks, frogs and small animals. Ask your teacher if your school yard can go wild. Or try other growing projects. Here are some ideas.

PLANTS WITHOUT DIRT

You may think all plants need soil to survive. Actually, some plants die when they are put in soil. They prefer to grow on air or in water. Here's how to grow some "air plants."

You'll need:

a pot
sand
a trellis
small stones or gravel

sphagnum moss
    (get some at your florist)
garbage bag ties
ivy
a water mister

1. Fill a pot with sand. Put the trellis in the pot and surround it with stones for support.

2. Wrap the moss around the trellis in several places and tie it on with garbage bag ties.

3. Attach the ivy to the moss on the trellis with garbage bag ties.

4. Mist with water and watch your plants grow on air!

NO-FUSS GARDENS

A cactus garden is probably the easiest garden to tend. Cactuses are used to being ignored! Fill a shallow clay pot with sandy soil. (You probably even have a clay pot you made at camp sitting around.) Plant different kinds of cactus — the hairy kind is called Old Man cactus, the Hedge cactus looks like a cucumber and the Golden Ball cactus looks like its name. It's easy to take cuttings from someone's cactus. Just cut off the shoots at the bottom of the big cactus. Let them dry for a few days before planting. Put some stones around the plants, water lightly and put in a hot, sunny place.

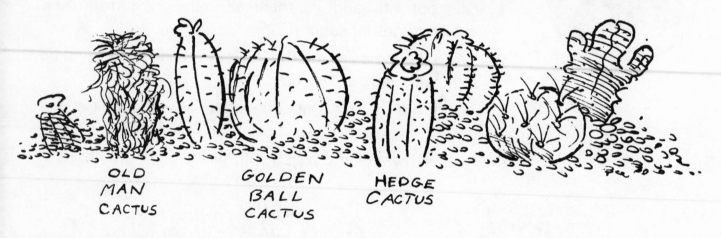

OLD MAN CACTUS   GOLDEN BALL CACTUS   HEDGE CACTUS

Grow a no-fuss weed garden by collecting floating seeds from the air or ground. Use an old milk carton or can (poke a few holes in the bottom for drainage), add some potting soil then your seeds. Cover the seeds with a layer of soil and water well. You may discover some beautiful weeds.

POKE HOLES IN BOTTOM

seeds   Potting soil

WATER

Plant sunflower seeds in a hot, sunny place. You'll not only attract birds, but you'll have some great tasting seeds to roast at the end of the summer. (Give seeds to all your friends and see who has the tallest sunflower at the end of the summer.)

Rain forests thrive on heat and rain. To make a miniature version, you'll need a large glass bottle with a lid or a fish tank and a piece of glass that covers the top. Put a layer of gravel and charcoal (from your fireplace or camp fire) on the bottom, cover with a rich layer of compost or topsoil and plant three or four exotic plants. (Inexpensive ones are available at your florist or supermarket.) Water well, put on the lid and put your mini–rain forest in a sunny place. And here's the surprise — you won't have to water again for a couple of months. Can you figure out why?

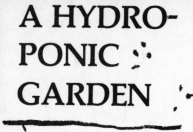

A HYDRO-PONIC GARDEN

In the late 1920s an American scientist named Dr. Gericke first used the word hydroponics (from the Greek word, hydro, for water and ponus, meaning work). Hydroponically grown plants use no soil. They are "planted" in gravel, sand, marble or vermiculite. Instead of getting nutrients from soil, hydroponic plants are fed nutrient-rich water.

In large hydroponic farms, water enriched with minerals is pumped through plastic pipes to each plant. The best part of hydroponic growing is that farmers never have to worry about soil diseases or weeds. It's also a wonderful way for farmers in poor soil areas to grow terrific fruits and vegetables. The problem is that once a disease attacks one plant, it can spread within hours to all the plants in the farm.

Why not give hydroponics a try? You might want to plant two identical plants — one in soil and the other in marbles or pebbles. Water them and watch them grow. For this activity, you can use plain water. If you really get into hydroponics, your garden centre can sell you a nutrient solution to add to your water.

You'll need:

a deep bowl
pebbles or marbles
3 hyacinth bulbs or 3 narcissus bulbs
    (ones with a bit of green showing are best)
water

1. Cover the bottom of the bowl with a 5 cm (2-inch) layer of pebbles or marbles.

2. Put the bulbs in so that the pointy ends are up. Make sure the bulbs are snugly embedded in the pebbles.

3. Pour in water until it reaches the bottom of the bulbs. Don't cover the bulbs in water or they'll rot. Don't put in too little water or the bulbs will die of thirst!

4. Put the bulbs in a cool, dark place for 4 weeks.

5. Keep checking the water. Make sure the bottom of the bulbs always have something to drink.

6. When the dish is filled with roots, put the bulbs in a sunny window and watch the water level. Soon you'll have stunning flowers to enjoy.
   P.S. If you start in the fall when the bulbs are in the stores, you'll have a wonderful present to give during the holidays!

GROWING NATURALLY

When you nibble a carrot or munch into an apple, the last thing you worry about are the chemicals you might be eating. Farmers use chemicals in growing to get rid of unwanted bugs and to make the produce grow bigger and look better. Producers may coat your fruits and vegetables with chemicals so they stay fresher longer. Apples and cucumbers aren't shiny when they come off the tree and vine — that's a wax you're eating!

Some people want food grown naturally — without any chemicals. There's a small price to pay — it costs more to eat organic food because it is not plentiful in the stores (yet!), and the fruits and vegetables do not look perfect.

So how do farmers grow organically? They use compost and manure for fertilizer instead of chemicals. They get rid of bugs with other bugs. (A bug that eats one crop may be a tasty treat for another bug.) Farmers can also use flowers to control bugs. For example, the odour of marigolds is so stinky to some bugs and small animals that they leave nearby crops alone. And farmers make sure the ground is kept rich in minerals and nutrients by moving the crops around from season to season. Peas and beans put minerals into the soil, but wheat and barley gobble minerals up.

If everybody asked for organic food at stores, there would be a larger market for the produce and the price would drop.

GROW A HIDEAWAY

Next time you need a place to get away from it all, why not grow it? You can grow a leafy and edible house with runner pole beans. And if you buy the scarlet runner bean seeds, which sprout into brilliant red flowers, you might attract hummingbirds.

You'll need:

a large garden spot with good soil
6 poles or pieces of dowling, each 2 m
    (6 feet) long
strong string
runner pole bean seeds
a supply of water

1. Make a tee-pee shape with the poles. Push the ends of the poles into the ground. Get a friend to help you tie the tops together with heavy string.

2. Tie string between each pole so the bean vines can grab onto something. Don't forget to leave a hole so you can get into your hideaway.

3. Plant three or four seeds at the base of each pole. Cover them with about 2.5 cm (1 inch) of dirt.

4. The vines will grow along the strings and cover your frame. When you crawl in, you can see without being seen.

ANSWERS

Plant's best friend (page 58)

1 *False*. Earthworms have male and female organs but they must mate with another earthworm to reproduce. After the worms exchange sperm, each parent worm secretes a slime ring around its body and the fertilized egg. The parent slithers out of the slime. The slime hardens into an egg case and in 30 to 100 days, a baby earthworm emerges.

2 *False*. Earthworms breathe through their skins. They must stay moist or they die.

3 *True*. And more in lush garden soil.

4 *False*. If you cut an earthworm in the middle — anywhere from the fourth to the twenty-third segment — it will die. But if the worm is cut in the very first or very last segments, it will grow a new head or a new tail. One earthworm managed to grow a new head 21 times in a lab experiment.

5 *True*. They dig below the frost line and spend a cozy winter.

6 *True*. In Australia, 4-m (12-foot) earthworms slither underground and make a sound like a giant bathtub draining.

7 *True*. After a heavy rain, the earthworms' burrows fill with water and the worms slither up to the surface. In the olden days, people just saw the wet worms and drew the wrong conclusion.

8 *True*.

9 *False*. Earthworms have clinging little legs called setae on each segment. These setae grab hold tightly to the burrow walls.

My mummy, the mummy (page 33)
The brains were taken out through the nose.

GLOSSARY

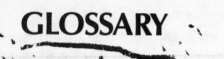

Archaeology: the science of studying how people lived in the past.

Bacteria: microscopic plants. Some cause disease; others cause decay.

Decompose: rot or decay.

Erosion: the changing of river banks, mountains and other land forms by natural forces such as wind and water.

Geology: the science of studying the rocks that make up the earth's crust.

Hazardous waste: garbage that could harm people, animals or the environment.

Humus: an ingredient of soil made from decayed plants and animals.

Magma: liquid rock under the earth's crust.

Minerals: the basic ingredients of rocks.

Molecules: the tiny building blocks of all things.

Organic growing or farming: growing foods without chemical fertilizers or pest killers.

Parasite: a plant or animal that lives on another plant or animal to survive.

Sediment: solids that have been deposited by wind, water or glaciers.

Topsoil: the top layer of soil that has the nutrients (food) plants need for growing.

Weathering: the natural wearing down of rocks into dirt.

INDEX